M000302946

Book of Love

A gift of appreciation to remind someone they're remarkable

Fill this book with something you saw, felt or loved about someone, every day for 30 days. The practice will make you more present and deepen your relationship. Then this book becomes a gift for them.

Icons by Przemyslaw Kowski, Kristina Margaryan. Tatyana, Valeriia Vlasovtseva, Kareemovic, ME, my.taa, Olena Panasovska, MD Riduwan Molla

For ages 6 and up

Nonfiction
Body, Mind & Spirit / Inspiration & Personal Growth
Body, Mind & Spirit / Mindfulness
Family & Relationship / Love & Romance
Family & Relationship / Marriage & Long-Term Relationships
Self-Help / Motivational & Inspirational
Self-Help / Journaling
Self-Help / Spiritual

First Edition
Published by J.C. Baldwin
www.jcbaldwin.net

In Appreciation

We're so fortunate to have people that warm our lives and make us smile. Yet they don't always know how much they mean to us. And even though they're cherished, they sometimes feel unseen. The moments of joy may be many, but the openings to acknowledge them can be few.

That's the first reason for this book, to capture some of that love shining through and reflect it back to them with deep appreciation.

The second is to help us clarify ourselves. The daily practice of creating this book can establish a rhythm of appreciation that helps us to better enjoy being present with our relationships, our self and our world.

When we take a moment to appreciate the gift in front of us, we create an opening. And that spaciousness invites expansion... consciousness... renewal... forgiveness... healing... transformation.

Please receive the gift of this journey with love for your relationship, your companions, and yourself. May it have the same profound impact it's had on myself and my family. And if you find it helpful, consider leaving a review. That will help others find it as well.

-- J.C. Baldwin

Creating a Book of Love

Pick a time of day when you can take a moment of appreciation for someone you love. (You may want to set a phone alarm as a daily reminder; though you might find yourself writing at other times as well.)

At least once a day write down glimpses of the love that expresses in their presence. (You can add a few at a time, if you're in a flow. Fond memories are also great. You have 50 entries to allow for both. *Some sample entries can be found in the appendix, and a QR link if you prefer to work from your devices.*)

30 days is about what the process was designed to take, though it can take more or less. The important thing is to establish a daily rhythm of appreciating someone.

Then this book becomes a gift to remind the person they're remarkable.

And a practice that will deepen the relationship the two of you share, and your connection to yourself.

A few things to get you thinking on this journey:

Don't you just love the way that person can...
and always seems to...
and has a great knack for...
and always makes you feel...
and how they can fill you with wonder...
and their dedication...
kindness... creativity...surprises...
support...sense of humor...
respect...patience...authenticity...
generosity...forgiveness...
affection...

and why have you been given
the great gift of this person in your life?

We're here to love; it's really that simple.
Now go write the book of love.

These reflections have been
gathered for:

_____

A gift from:

_____

Date: _____

I love that you are:

_____

_____

Like the moment:

_____

_____

_____

_____

_____

Date: _____

I love that you are:

_____

_____

Like the moment:

_____

_____

_____

_____

_____

_____

Date: _____

I love that you are:

_____

_____

Like the moment:

_____

_____

_____

_____

_____

_____

Date: _____

I love that you are:

_____

_____

Like the moment:

_____

_____

_____

_____

_____

"The only thing we never get enough of is love; and the only thing we never give enough of is love."
—Henry Miller

"Where there is great love, there are always miracles."
—Willa Cather

Date: _____

I love that you are:

_____

_____

Like the moment:

_____

_____

_____

_____

_____

_____

Date: _____

I love that you are:

_____

_____

Like the moment:

_____

_____

_____

_____

_____

_____

Date: _____

I love that you are:

_____

_____

Like the moment:

_____

_____

_____

_____

_____

Date: _____

I love that you are:

_____

_____

Like the moment:

_____

_____

_____

_____

_____

_____

Date: _____

I love that you are:

_____

_____

Like the moment:

_____

_____

_____

_____

_____

_____

Date: _____

I love that you are:

_____

_____

Like the moment:

_____

_____

_____

_____

_____

_____

10

Kind **yummy**
dedicated **gentle**
sweet soulful
smart loving
considerate **sexy**
thoughtful funny
soft exceptional
caring honoring
beautiful youthful
respectful **happy**

Date: _____

I love that you are:

_____

_____

Like the moment:

_____

_____

_____

_____

_____

_____

Date: _____

I love that you are:

_____

_____

Like the moment:

_____

_____

_____

_____

_____

_____

Date: _____

I love that you are:

_____

_____

Like the moment:

_____

_____

_____

_____

_____

_____

Date: _____

I love that you are:

_____

_____

Like the moment:

_____

_____

_____

_____

_____

"Passion makes the world go 'round.
Love just makes it a safer place."
—Ice-T

"*Your task is not to seek for love, but merely to seek and find all the barriers within yourself that you have built against it.*"
—Rumi

Date: _____

I love that you are:

_____

_____

Like the moment:

_____

_____

_____

_____

_____

_____

Date: _____

I love that you are:

_____

_____

Like the moment:

_____

_____

_____

_____

_____

_____

Date: _____

I love that you are:

_____

_____

Like the moment:

_____

_____

_____

_____

_____

Date: _____

I love that you are:

_____

_____

Like the moment:

_____

_____

_____

_____

_____

_____

Date: _____

I love that you are:

_____

_____

Like the moment:

_____

_____

_____

_____

_____

_____

Date: _____

I love that you are:

_____

_____

Like the moment:

_____

_____

_____

_____

_____

_____

20

cheerful exciting
energetic **colorful**
deserving strong
sincere **creative**
honest charming
reliable **bright**
resourceful
trusting capable
supportive **willing**
affectionate
powerful **forgiving**

Date: _____

I love that you are:

_____

_____

Like the moment:

_____

_____

_____

_____

_____

_____

Date: _____

I love that you are:

_____

_____

Like the moment:

_____

_____

_____

_____

_____

_____

Date: _____

I love that you are:

_____

_____

Like the moment:

_____

_____

_____

_____

_____

_____

Date: _____

I love that you are:

_____

_____

Like the moment:

_____

_____

_____

_____

_____

_____

"Sometimes love breaks our heart to open it."
—JC Baldwin

"The greatest happiness of life is the conviction that we are loved; loved for ourselves, or rather, loved in spite of ourselves"
—Victor Hugo

Date: _____

I love that you are:

_____

_____

Like the moment:

_____

_____

_____

_____

_____

_____

Date: _____

I love that you are:

_____

_____

Like the moment:

_____

_____

_____

_____

_____

_____

Date: _____

I love that you are:

_____

_____

Like the moment:

_____

_____

_____

_____

_____

_____

Date: _____

I love that you are:

_____

_____

Like the moment:

_____

_____

_____

_____

_____

_____

Date: _____

I love that you are:

_____

_____

Like the moment:

_____

_____

_____

_____

_____

_____

Date: _____

I love that you are:

_____

_____

Like the moment:

_____

_____

_____

_____

_____

30

resourceful
trusting thoughtful
supportive kind
affectionate sexy
powerful **bright**
forgiving colorful
willing capable
gentle sweet
dedicated **soulful**
loving considerate
yummy

Date: _____

I love that you are:

_____

_____

Like the moment:

_____

_____

_____

_____

_____

Date: _____

I love that you are:

_____

_____

Like the moment:

_____

_____

_____

_____

_____

_____

Date: _____

I love that you are:

_____

_____

Like the moment:

_____

_____

_____

_____

_____

Date: _____

I love that you are:

_____

_____

Like the moment:

_____

_____

_____

_____

_____

_____

"Love sometimes wants to do us a great favor: hold us upside down and shake all the nonsense out."
—Rumi

*"We tend to think love is something that finds us.
Maybe if we're in the right place at the right time,
love will bump into us and we'll meet it. But how
can love be something that plays hide and seek outside of us,
if it rushes from the depths of our being?
We can feel it in music and see it in Earth's creatures.
When we are awake to love, it shows us to be limitless.
And this is how the saints live, as a vessel for love
pouring from within them... endlessly...
to whomever it can reach."*
—JC Baldwin

Date: _____

I love that you are:

_____

_____

Like the moment:

_____

_____

_____

_____

_____

_____

Date: _____

I love that you are:

_____

_____

Like the moment:

_____

_____

_____

_____

_____

_____

Date: _____

I love that you are:

_____

_____

Like the moment:

_____

_____

_____

_____

_____

_____

Date: _____

I love that you are:

_____

_____

Like the moment:

_____

_____

_____

_____

_____

_____

Date: _____

I love that you are:

_____

_____

Like the moment:

_____

_____

_____

_____

_____

_____

Date: _____

I love that you are:

_____

_____

Like the moment:

_____

_____

_____

_____

_____

_____

40

caring funny
exceptional **soft**
honoring
beautiful youthful
sincere
respectful **happy**
smart cheerful
exciting energetic
deserving **strong**
creative **honest**
charming reliable

Date: _____

I love that you are:

_____

_____

Like the moment:

_____

_____

_____

_____

_____

Date: _____

I love that you are:

_____

_____

Like the moment:

_____

_____

_____

_____

_____

_____

Date: _____

I love that you are:

_____

_____

Like the moment:

_____

_____

_____

_____

_____

_____

Date: _____

I love that you are:

_____

_____

Like the moment:

_____

_____

_____

_____

_____

"Love is that condition in which the happiness of another person is essential to your own." —Robert A. Heinlein

"Have enough courage to trust love one more time and always one more time." —Maya Angelou

Date: _____

I love that you are:

_____

_____

Like the moment:

_____

_____

_____

_____

_____

_____

Date: _____

I love that you are:

_____

_____

Like the moment:

_____

_____

_____

_____

_____

_____

Date: _____

I love that you are:

_____

_____

Like the moment:

_____

_____

_____

_____

_____

_____

Date: _____

I love that you are:

_____

_____

Like the moment:

_____

_____

_____

_____

_____

Date: _____

I love that you are:

_____

_____

Like the moment:

_____

_____

_____

_____

_____

_____

Date: _____

I love that you are:

_____

_____

Like the moment:

_____

_____

_____

_____

_____

_____

50

Something I received from writing about you:

_____

_____

_____

_____

_____

_____

_____

_____

"True love stories never have endings."
—Richard Bach

To be continued…

Appendix

Pencil to Paper

This practice was developed to establish a rhythm of appreciation in your life. Detailed, daily reflections help you to be more mindful and present on your journey. But our relationships are also anchored in many fond memories as well.

With this in mind, it's okay to fill your first pages with recollections that capture the person you love and admire. The book is designed to give you room for this. You can also add more memories when you recall them along the way.

Samples

To get an idea of different approaches, here are some sample entries that people have shared:

I love that you are: *cozy.*

Like the moment: *you hugged me for a really long time this morning, and I didn't want to let go. And your sweater was extra soft, which made your hug even cozier.*

I love that you are: *the glue that holds our family together.*

Like the moment: *the kids were younger and we were folding laundry together, and you turned it into a game with the kids. It became fun and happy. It felt like we were sharing some great secret to life.*

Digital Notebook

When you fill a Book of Love with your own words, written in your own handwriting, you create a gift that can be cherished for years to come.

In the event that you prefer the convenience of making your notes on your phone or computer, or you want to capture your thoughts while they're fresh even if you don't have the book with you, here is a link to an electronic notepad that can be copied and pasted into electronic note taking formats. *(This will work for Google Docs, Apple Notes, etc.)*

Every week, or when you've completed your appreciation practice, you can then take some time, perhaps over a few days, to copy your digital entries into your Book of Love.

Scan for digital pages

http://tiny.cc/bookoflovepages

Instructions: Select all the text, copy it, then paste it into a new page in the app you use for note taking.

Printed in the USA
CPSIA information can be obtained
at www.ICGtesting.com
LVHW022150141023
761116LV00005B/108

9 780998 899213